WILDLIFE AT RISK

ENDANGERED BLUE WHALES

Jane Katirgis and Chris Reiter

 Enslow Publishing
101 W. 23rd Street
Suite 240
New York, NY 10011
USA

enslow.com

Published in 2016 by Enslow Publishing, LLC.
101 W. 23rd Street, Suite 240, New York, NY 10011

Library of Congress Cataloging-in-Publication Data

Katirgis, Jane, author.
 Endangered blue whales / Jane Katirgis and Chris Reiter.
    pages cm. — (Wildlife at risk)
 Summary: "Discusses blue whales, why they are endangered, and how they are being helped"-- Provided by publisher.
 Audience: Ages 11+
 Audience: Grades 7 to 8
 Includes bibliographical references and index.
 ISBN 978-0-7660-6890-2 (library binding)
 ISBN 978-0-7660-6888-9 (pbk.)
 ISBN 978-0-7660-6889-6 (6-pack)
 1. Blue whale—Juvenile literature. 2. Whales—Juvenile literature. 3. Rare mammals—Juvenile literature. I. Reiter, Chris, author. II. Title.
 QL737.C424K37 2016
 599.5'248—dc23
                          2015009975

Printed in the United States of America

To Our Readers: We have done our best to make sure all Web site addresses in this book were active and appropriate when we went to press. However, the author and the publisher have no control over and assume no liability for the material available on those Web sites or on any Web sites they may link to. Any comments or suggestions can be sent by e-mail to customerservice@enslow.com.

Portions of this book originally appeared in the book *The Blue Whale*.

Photos Credits: Brian J. Skerry/National Geographic/Getty Images, p. 35; Carol Grant/Moment Select/Getty images, p. 13; Creativ Studio Heinemann/Creative (RF)/Getty Images, p. 1 (borage flowers); David Tipling/Photographer's Choice/Getty images, p. 8; Fred Duval/FilmMagic/Getty Images, p. 39; Hakan Karlsson/Vetta/Getty Images, p. 37; hudiemm/E+/Getty Images (notebook fact boxes throughout book); Jeff Rotman/Stone/Getty Images, p.15; Joakim Leroy/E+/Getty Images, p. 1 (palm leaf); Maria Toutoudaki/Photodisk/Getty Images (background paper texture throughout book); Mark Carwardine/Photolibrary/Getty images, p.7; Mark Conlin/Oxford Scientific/Getty Images, p. 41; PATRICK HAMILTON/AFP/Getty Images, p. 33; SCIEPRO/Science Photo Library/Getty Images, pp. 1 (blue whale), 18; Stringer/Anadolu Agency/Getty Images, p. 26.

Cover Credits: SCIEPRO/Science Photo Library/Getty Images (blue whale); oakim Leroy/E+/Getty images (palm leaf); Creativ Studio Heinemann/Creative (RF)/Getty Images (borage flowers); Maria Toutoudaki/Photodisk/Getty Images (background paper texture).

CONTENTS

Blue Whales at a Glance

Class

Mammalia

Family

Balaenopteridae

Genus

Balaenoptera

Species

musculus

Average Length

70 to 100 feet (21 to 30 meters)
Females are about 5 percent longer than males.

Average Weight

100 to 120 tons (91 to 109 metric tons)

Life Span

More than 80 years

Status

Listed by the United States Fish and Wildlife Service (USFWS) as endangered on June 2, 1970.

Skin Color

Bluish gray and mottled with gray and white
Underside yellowish or whitish

Teeth

Baleen (whalebone) strips extending from 270 to 395 plates in the jaw.

Breeding Season

Midwinter months

Gestation Period

11 to 12 months

Offspring

One every 2 to 3 years

Range

Worldwide; separate northern and southern stocks

Maximum Speed

Faster than 19 mph (30 kph)

Threats to Survival

Hunting by humans, habitat loss, pollution, competition with humans for food

Voice

Low, rumbling, often arranged in patterns

Spout

Up to 30 feet (9 meters) high

chapter one

THE LARGEST ANIMAL

Here's a question for you: What animal weighs more than ten adult elephants and has a heart the size of a smart car? The answer is the largest animal that has ever lived on earth. This animal is also quite hungry. It eats the equivalent of about 32,000 hamburgers in just a day.[1] That is a serious appetite.

A creature so big and with an appetite so enormous surely has to be the hulking, meat-eating *Tyrannosaurus rex* or the towering *Apatosaurus*. But in fact, the world's largest animal ever is not an extinct dinosaur. It is alive today and swimming in all the world's oceans. It is the giant of the sea, the blue whale.

Just how big is the blue whale? Let's go back to the heart. It's as large as a small car because it must move blood the entire length of the whale's long, streamlined body, which is an astonishing 100 feet (30 meters). It would take twenty schoolchildren lying end to end in a straight line to equal the length of the blue whale. An average first-grader could actually crawl through the whale's aorta, the large artery that carries blood from the whale's heart to the rest of its body. Each beat of the blue whale's heart pumps 60 gallons (227 liters) of blood into the aorta![2]

A Whale's Diet

Such a huge animal needs a lot of food to keep it going. One might think that a blue whale would eat a few big fish every day to satisfy its hunger. But the whale's diet is made up almost entirely of a tiny,

A 22-foot (7-meter) boat looks like a small toy next to a blue whale. The blue whale is an endangered species despite its size—and because of it. One blue whale provides much more blubber, whalebone, and oil than several smaller whales.

shrimplike creature called krill. Trying to get full on krill is like trying to make three square meals out of a swarm of gnats—one would need to eat a lot of them. That's just what the blue whale does. During its six-month feeding season in the cold polar seas, it devours 40 million krill every day—an amazing 8,000 pounds (3,629 kilograms) of krill![3] This is a very, very big animal.

The blue whale's size gives it many advantages. Large animals stay warm more easily than small ones and tend to expend less

Krill are tiny shrimplike creatures that serve as the main food source for the enormous blue whale. Conservationists are now concerned that global warning is causing ice melts in the seas where krill live and blue whales feed, which would further endanger the species.

energy feeding. Blue whales also have few predators. Killer whales, also known as orcas, sometimes attack young blue whale calves, but mature blue whales are rarely threatened. Even fierce sharks stay away from the mighty blue whale.

Their great size also gives blue whales a powerful voice. They make deep rumbling sounds that travel for hundreds of miles across the ocean. The sound is something like that of a foghorn or a tuba played underwater. Scientists believe that the blue whale's calls are a way of communicating with other whales. As blue whales search for krill, for instance, a resounding bellow may tell other whales where to find a good meal.

Whales as Prey

Unfortunately, great size has its disadvantages, too. For centuries, ocean hunters coveted the blue whale. When they spotted a big blue whale swimming the open seas, they saw an unmatched source of meat, oil, and whalebone. Before electricity, whale oil was burned in lanterns to provide light. Whale meat was an important part of the diet of many people. Whalebone was used in corsets and umbrellas. Whalers could make a profit from selling those products. But the early whalers were no match for the powerful, swift-swimming blue whale. Their open rowboats were too slow, and their hand-held harpoons were too weak. Late in the nineteenth century, however, whalers began to use fast steam-powered boats, harpoon cannons, and exploding harpoons. By 1900, whalers were killing thousands of blue whales each year. In 1931, more than 29,000 blue whales were killed in a single season.[4]

Whaling

Modern commercial whaling nearly wiped out the world's population of blue whales. Scientists estimate that a population of 250,000 that lived before whaling began was reduced to fewer than 10,000.[5] Some believe the numbers dropped as low as 2,000.

Ten thousand whales might sound like a lot, but whalers killed almost three times that number in a single season. That is why blue whales are an endangered species—a species that is in danger of becoming extinct.

The International Whaling Commission

Blue whales have been considered an endangered species since 1966. They had become so scarce by then that the International Whaling Commission (IWC) declared an end to the hunting of the great whale. The IWC is the agency responsible for the regulation of the whaling industry and the conservation of whales.

The United States is a member nation of the IWC. In addition to following the IWC ban, the United States has passed laws that protect whales and other species at risk.

In 1972, Congress passed the Marine Mammal Protection Act, which banned fishing for all whales, dolphins, and porpoises in US waters. In 1973, Congress passed the Endangered Species

Act, which combined and strengthened the provisions of earlier endangered species acts. It provides for the conservation of all domestic and foreign animal and plant species that are endangered. Once a species is listed under the act as endangered or threatened, that species receives protection under the law. Along with listing the blue whale, the act listed seven other species of whales that had been hunted to near extinction: the gray whale, bowhead whale, fin or finback whale, humpback whale, northern right whale, sei whale, and sperm whale.

Hope for the Future

Today, whales are enjoying a modest recovery. The population of gray whales has recovered so well that they are no longer considered endangered. You can even watch gray whales migrate off the west coast of North America. They swim from the shores of the Baja California peninsula in Mexico all the way north to Alaska. Many blue whales follow a similar route. They can be seen during the summer and autumn in the waters off the central California coast. Scientists have counted up to 2,000 blue whales there. It is the largest concentration of blue whales in the world.[6]

chapter two

A Look at the Whale

Considering how large they are and that they live in the ocean, it may be hard to believe that whales and humans are close relatives. They both are mammals, though. There are about five thousand different species, or individual types, of mammals. Mammals have many common traits. They breathe air, and they have well-developed brains and warm blood. Female mammals produce milk for their young. A mammal's entire body has a sense of touch. Most of the other sense organs are located in a mammal's head.

Sea Mammals

Most mammals have a coat of hair all over their bodies. But some mammals, specifically those that live at least some of the time in the water, do not have much hair at all. These are the marine mammals.

There are three main groups of marine mammals: pinnipeds, sirenians, and cetaceans. Seals, sea lions, fur seals, and walruses are all pinnipeds. Of the three groups, pinnipeds have the most hair because they spend a lot of time on land, as well as in the water.

Usually this is in colder temperatures, and they need hair for warmth, as well as for protection from being cut by rocks.

The sirenians, or sea cows, make up the second group of marine mammals. These peaceful animals spend almost all of their lives in shallow coastal waters or rivers. Sirenians eat underwater plants and grow to be quite large. The largest sirenian, the Steller's sea cow, was known to grow up to almost 25 feet (8 meters) in length, but it is now extinct. The other sea cows, the manatee and

Manatees, which live in shallow coastal waters and rivers, belong to the group of marine mammals known as sea cows. Of the three species of manatees alive today, two are endangered and one is threatened.

the dugong, are also increasingly rare.[1] The manatee, which can grow up to 13 feet (4 meters) long and weigh up to 1,300 pounds (590 kilograms), lives along the southeastern coast of the United States, as well as in coastal waters off Central America, the West Indies, northern South America, and western Africa. Dugongs are found in the tropical and subtropical waters of the Indian and Pacific Oceans, but most are found in the waters off Australia. The sea cows, despite their size, are so graceful that many believe the legend of the mermaid is based on them.[2]

Whales, dolphins, and porpoises belong to the third group of marine mammals, the cetaceans. There are seventy-eight known species of cetaceans and probably more that we do not know about.[3] Though the characteristics of cetaceans vary greatly, they all have the same general body shape, which is basically rounded and larger at the front than at the back. They also all have nostrils on the top of their head, no hind limbs, and a flat horizontal blade at the end of their tails, which makes them nimble swimmers. Marine biologists who have touched cetaceans say their skin is usually very smooth.[4]

Whales With Teeth

Less pleasing to touch is the equipment in a cetacean's mouth. Sixty-seven species of cetaceans have teeth and are therefore called toothed whales. All dolphins and porpoises are in this group, as are several types of whales.[5] These animals survive in the water by hunting fish and squid that are much smaller—usually between a hundred and a thousand times smaller—than they are.[6]

Dolphins belong to the group of marine mammals called cetaceans.

Blue Whales and Other Baleen Whales

The remaining eleven whale species make up a class all their own. They are called baleen whales, and they do not have teeth. Instead, they have long strips of bone, called baleen, along the insides of their mouths. Baleen is made of keratin, which is a substance like that of human fingernails.[7] The baleen changes in size from the back to the front of the jaw with the outermost strips being fine and flexible like the bristles of a broom or brush. In fact, when whales were commonly hunted, their baleen were used to make just these things.[8]

Baleen whales are filter feeders. When they are feeding, they swim through shoals, or large groups, of prey. They take in enormous gulps of water, which they then expel through their baleen while capturing thousands of krill, the small, shrimplike creatures that form most of their diet.[9]

Krill occur in "astonishing abundance" in the cold Southern Ocean (an ocean formed by the southern portions of the Atlantic, Pacific, and Indian Oceans), where they are also eaten by certain seals, penguins, squid, and fish.[10] They can grow to be 2.5 inches (6.3 centimeters) in length, which is between a million and a hundred million times smaller than the whales that eat them.[11]

Rorquals

Seven types of baleen whales are referred to as the rorquals. These whales have a series of pleats, or grooves, running along their throats and bellies. The name *rorqual* is from the Old Norse *rorhval,* meaning "grooved whales."[12] The individual species of

Fast Fact!

The tongue of a blue whale can weigh as much as an elephant! Although a blue whale would never eat people, one hundred humans could fit in its mouth.

rorqual whales are the humpback, fin, sei, Bryde's, minke, pygmy blue, and blue whales.

The blue whale, *Balaenoptera musculus*, is the largest of the rorquals. Females are generally larger than males of the same age, and the largest known blue whale was a female killed in the late 1920s near the South Shetland Islands off the tip of the Antarctic Peninsula. She was an astonishing 109 feet 4 inches (33 meters 10 centimeters) long. The largest male came from the same waters at around the same time. He was 107 feet 1 inch (32 meters 3 inches) long.[13] Even the largest dinosaurs would have looked small standing next to those creatures.

Blue whales are named for their color. The tops of their heads, backs, and tails are blue to bluish gray, sometimes with gray patches. Their bellies are lighter, usually yellowish or whitish, and the undersides of their bellies are white. Blue whales are sometimes called sulfur bottoms because a light film of algae that grows on their undersides reflects bright yellow.[14] Their baleen, which grows from almost 400 plates on each side of the upper jaw, are black. The longest known fibers of baleen have measured almost 4 feet (1 meter) long.[15]

In the water, a blue whale is usually easy to tell from other whales. Besides its color, its size gives it away. You can be pretty sure you are looking at a blue whale if the animal is longer than 75 feet (23 meters)—a good deal longer than an average school bus. Blue whales can weigh up to an immense 150 tons (136 metric tons).[16]

Blue whales are baleen whales—instead of teeth, they have long strips of bone in their mouths called baleen that filter water and strain food.

The pygmy blue whale, a variant of the blue whale, was first written about in 1961. It is most commonly seen in the Southern Ocean, especially in the Indian Ocean near the Kerguelen Islands. Even though pygmy implies a small size, female pygmy blue whales can reach a length of almost 80 feet (24 meters) and males about 70 feet (21 meters).[17]

Blue Whale Migration and Krill

Wherever there are oceans, there are whales. Blue whales are found worldwide in two separate groups that do not interbreed. One group lives in the northern seas, and the other group lives in the southern seas. Although some whales stay in the same general area for their entire lives, blue whales migrate and travel long distances between feeding and wintering waters.

Blue whales spend the summer months of each year in frigid polar seas. The northern stocks migrate to the Arctic region, and the southern stocks swim to the Antarctic. This movement is tied to the polar food bloom, when krill are plentiful and multiplying.[18] Blue whales feed intensively during these months, gorging on krill, and put on lots of weight. As much as one ton of food has been found in a blue whale's stomach during the peak of the feeding season.

Krill do not reproduce in the exact same spot every year, but blue whales seem to be able to use their powerful voices to let one another know where to feed. Once they find a shoal of krill, blue whales have several ways of making the krill swim closer together so they can swallow more krill in each mouthful. Blue whales sometimes dive beneath the shoals, swim in circles, and release bubbles as they go. As the bubbles float upward, they confuse the krill, which react by swimming closer together for protection. Then the whales swim through the center of the group and eat many, many krill.[19]

Scientists are not sure why the krill do not swim through the bubbles, but the whales' feeding style is so effective that it is called bubble netting. Scientists have observed teams of whales working together to form very large bubble nets. When whales work

Fast Fact!

Blue whales make noises that are louder than jet engines. They can hear each other from up to 1,000 miles (1,600 kilometers) away.

together like this, it is widely believed that they coordinate their actions with special sounds.[20]

Krill usually have little luck trying to swim away from whales, though, because whales are fast swimmers. While feeding, whales swim from 1 to 4 mph (2 to 6.5 kph), and their normal cruising speed while migrating through the open ocean is between 3 and 8 mph (5 and 14 kph). When pursued or wounded, whales have been known to swim up to 20 mph (30 kph).[21] After taking a deep breath on the surface, a whale can dive into the ocean and stay beneath the surface for twenty minutes or more.[22]

Time for Breeding

As winter comes and the polar food bloom ends, blue whales migrate thousands of miles to their breeding grounds, where whales couple and mate. Even the whales that are too young or too old to breed make the annual migration.

Once fertilized, a female blue whale carries her young for ten to eleven months. She seeks out calmer, warmer waters to give birth and does so in midwinter.[23] A fertile female blue whale usually gives birth to one infant, called a calf, every two to three years.

Like all mammals, blue whale calves nurse on their mother's milk. For the first few weeks of their lives, they can gain up to 250 pounds (113 kilograms) daily just from drinking milk! Because a lot of milk is lost into the water during the process of nursing, female whales sometimes produce up to 750 pounds (340 kilograms) of milk each day.[24]

Away from the polar waters, blue whales do not eat that much. Even their biggest gulps of food amount to no more than a tiny snack when compared to the huge mouthfuls of krill they swallow while in the icy polar waters. Because they store so much energy, blue whales and other baleen whales can fast, or go without eating, longer than most other animals.[25] Then as spring approaches, they are ready to head north again and continue the migratory rounds they have made for thousands of years.

chapter three

Threats to the Whale

Since before written history, humans have hunted whales. These sea mammals have been prized for their valuable oil and meat. For three to four thousand years, the native people in Alaska and the Arctic have hunted whales. To this day, they use boats called umiaks. These boats are made of sealskin stretched on a wooden frame.

In the past, once the whale was pulled ashore, the Alaska Natives would gather for many hours to pray and thank the whale for giving its life. It was then butchered, and the blubber, meat, and bones were all used—no parts of the whale were wasted. Only a few whales were killed each year, and the overall population of whales remained healthy.[1]

Past Whalers

The Norwegians have also eaten whale meat for thousands of years, although it is not known whether they originally hunted or scavenged for whales. The Japanese, too, have a long history of whaling with written records of whale hunts dating back to

1606. The first European whalers were the Basques (people from the western Pyrenees Mountains along the border of France and Spain), who were known to hunt whales in the Bay of Biscay as far back as the tenth century. These early hunters used small simple boats to track and chase whales. They would thrust a harpoon into a whale's back, and the whale would exhaust itself dragging the hunters' boat. The whalers would eventually pull alongside the tired whale and stab it with a long metal lance while hoping to puncture its heart or lungs.[2]

Whaling Today

During the second half of the nineteenth century, the methods and instruments used to hunt whales changed dramatically. In about 1864, a Norwegian named Svend Foyn invented a cannon that could be fixed onto the bow, or front, of a ship.[3] The cannon fired harpoons farther and faster than they could be fired by hand.

The cannons were mounted on steam-powered ships, which allowed whalers to reach the polar seas where whales congregate to feed each year. Whalers also learned that a whale could be pumped full of air to keep it from sinking. Before that discovery, whalers could only hunt whales that floated. But now whalers could hunt almost any whale and easily transport it back to port for processing.

Over the years, whalers established processing sites closer and closer to whale stocks. They also built factory ships on which they butchered, processed, and froze whales while still at sea. The factory ships would anchor near large icebergs, which blocked the fierce weather, while small boats called catchers did the actual hunting. When a catcher boat killed a whale, it towed the animal to the factory ship for processing. Technology was transforming traditional whaling into a fast-growing industry.

With advanced technology, whaling became even easier. Whalers began to use helicopters and other aircraft to spot whales from above. They also tracked whale movements with sonar, a device that uses the echoes of underwater sound waves to locate objects. When whalers discovered that a certain frequency of sonar caused whales to panic and surface, many ships began using that frequency.

Other modern whaling methods include the use of exploding harpoons, from which pieces of metal were blasted throughout a whale's body by an explosive charge in the harpoon's tip. When people became concerned that these explosions were wasting too much meat, whalers began to use cold harpoons. These were blunt metal tubes that could knock a whale unconscious or possibly kill it if they were fired into exactly the right spot. Whales were usually struck by several cold harpoons before they died.[4]

Fast Fact!

Blue whales can live in a group or alone. The largest group usually contains about sixty whales.

Chemical Threats

Whalers are not the only threat to whales. Many chemical products made by humans have been found to be extremely harmful to marine life, and the substances are still finding their way into ocean waters. Some of the most harmful chemicals are compounds known as organohalogens, which are commonly found in pesticides, insecticides, herbicides, and fungicides. While many organohalogens are no longer produced, they are still being released into the environment when disposed of improperly.

One type of organohalogen, polychlorinated biphenyl (PCB), is a fairly common pollutant. When whales feed on small animals with PCBs in their tissues, the chemical accumulates in the whales' flesh in high levels. That accumulation can lead to serious health problems for whales by affecting their ability to have offspring and weakening their immune systems. Even though PCBs are no longer produced, many nations still use existing supplies.

Fishing Threats

Many cetaceans also lose their lives each year in accidental killings when they get caught in fishing nets. Dolphins, for example, get caught in nets intended to catch tuna because tuna often swim beneath dolphins and follow them to sources of food.

Even greater numbers of cetaceans are believed to have drowned in drift nets, which are now banned worldwide by a United Nations declaration.[5] Drift nets are nearly invisible and highly flexible nets that trap any marine animal larger than the holes in the nets' mesh. Before being banned, drift nets were being used to catch more

A 65.6-foot (20-meter) dead blue whale washed ashore on Failaka Island in Kuwait on February 28, 2014.

fish than any other method of fishing. These nets were secured on either end by floats and sometimes extended up to 60 miles (96 kilometers). They were cast out at night when the fish could not see them and collected the following morning. In addition to catching nontarget fish, which were simply thrown away, drift nets accidentally killed hundreds of thousands of marine mammals each year, as well as large numbers of seabirds and sea turtles.[6]

Unfortunately, despite the ban, illegal fleets still use drift nets on the high seas.

Even More Threats

Whales face many other threats. They often die from collisions with seagoing vessels. Both large ships and small fishing boats can do serious harm to whales.[7] Of course, the reverse is also true—whales have been known to do serious damage to ships and even sink some of them.

Coastal development can also affect the lives of whales. Building that goes on in coastal areas causes small particles of sand and dirt, or sediment, to run off into the ocean. Sedimentation clouds the water, cuts off sunlight, and changes the flow of nutrients in the sea. Sometimes it changes the marine environment so much that coastal waters can't support many forms of aquatic life. Whales may depend on these life-forms. When development along the coast brings too many people to whale breeding grounds, whales have been known to avoid those areas.

Underwater noise is another cause for concern. Researchers believe whales use sound to navigate. When sonar, underwater

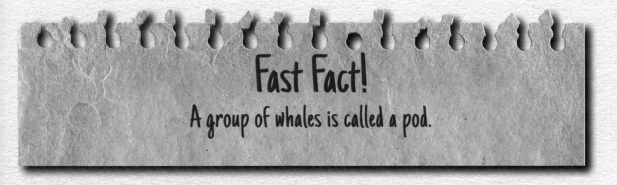

Fast Fact!
A group of whales is called a pod.

explosions from military testing, and the drone of underwater oil wells add strange new sounds to the sea, whales can become confused. Some scientists suspect that whales beach themselves on shorelines when underwater noise interferes with their navigation.

Whales With Purpose

Every creature in the ocean has a purpose even if we do not yet understand it, and all marine life is somehow interconnected. Some scientists have compared this relationship to the parts of a spider's web with each species being a strand of the web. When one strand is damaged, the strands that are connected are also harmed. If too many strands are frayed, the whole web may fall apart.

When we take too many creatures from our oceans, we run the risk of damaging the web of life. Many people realized this as they saw whales hunted to near extinction. They decided to do something about it.

chapter four
WATCHING OUT FOR WHALES

Almost one hundred years ago, people started to recognize that whales needed legal protection. Whales that were the most endangered in 1931 were protected by the Convention for the Regulation of Whaling. This international hunting ban protected gray, bowhead, and right whales. Most countries began to follow the restrictions in 1937, when the convention became a law. However, not all countries adhered to the restrictions on hunting these whales. The aboriginal peoples—the original inhabitants of an area—were still allowed to hunt gray and bowhead whales.

The outbreak of World War II gave whales a bit of rest because whaling in many areas ceased altogether. Many whaling vessels were torpedoed as countries fought over territory in the seas. In 1946, after the war, when whalers returned to the seas, the International Convention for the Regulation of Whaling was ratified in Washington, D.C. That same year, the International Whaling Commission (IWC) met for the first time.

Fast Fact!

As you may expect, the largest animal on earth has very large babies. A newborn blue whale is about 25 feet (8 meters) long and weighs 3 tons.

Hunting Regulations

The IWC began to monitor and regulate whaling worldwide, but in its early years the organization acted more to develop the whaling industry than to protect whales. By 1964, the total population of blue whales hovered under two thousand, and many people feared that the species would soon disappear from the earth.

In 1966 the IWC finally called for the end of blue whale hunting. Certain whaling countries, however, did not enter into the agreement. Peru and Chile, for example, continued hunting blue whales.

During the 1970s, the IWC began to more actively protect whales.[1] At the same time, the United States passed two laws that increased protections for all cetaceans. The first law was the 1972 Marine Mammal Protection Act, which banned fishing for whales, dolphins, and porpoises in US waters and made it illegal to import whale products into the United States. This feature of the act was important because whale oil was still being used to manufacture machine oil and cosmetics.[2]

The second law was the Endangered Species Act, passed by Congress in 1973, which established special protections for animals and plants in danger of disappearing from the earth. The act also protects threatened species, or those species considered likely to be in danger of extinction if they are not protected. Blue whales and seven other whale species were listed by the act as endangered.

A Halt to Commercial Whaling

In 1982, the IWC passed its boldest whale conservation action ever. It proclaimed a moratorium, or temporary halt, on all commercial whaling beginning in 1985. During the moratorium, the IWC reviewed its management policies to decide whether some whaling could be conducted at levels that would not devastate the future of the species.[3]

The IWC has no direct power to force nations to follow its rules, but many member nations have threatened economic sanctions against those countries that continue to hunt whales. Sanctions are measures that block trade with a country, which can affect its economic well-being. The United States has repeatedly

Fast Fact!

Blue whales can reach speeds of more than 19 miles (30 kilometers) an hour.

threatened sanctions against nations that break IWC rules but has rarely imposed sanctions over whaling concerns.[4]

The IWC rules allow nations to issue themselves permits to kill whales for scientific research. Japan, Iceland, and Norway have issued themselves such permits and continue to be criticized by the international community for doing so. Many conservationists see the permits as a way to get around the whaling moratorium because many of the research programs in those countries have not fully met IWC standards. There are also other effective methods of research that do not involve killing whales.

Whale Conservation

Conservationists believe that whaling must be stopped in order to prevent whales from becoming extinct. And when a species becomes extinct, all other species in an ecosystem are affected. Conservationists also argue that killing whales is unnecessary because there is no longer any need for products made from whales. There are good substitutes for whale oil, whalebone, and whale meat. Moreover, they say killing whales is inhumane—it causes great pain to a magnificent creature for no reason.[5]

There are also people against whaling who believe it is good business to promote healthy whale stocks. The total amount of money spent by people who travel out onto the oceans hoping to see whales has far surpassed the total money spent on whale products. One researcher found that in 1992 almost 3.5 million Americans and nearly 5 million people worldwide went on whale-watching expeditions.[6] But even the best intentions can have

Sea World marine rescue workers try to rescue a humpback whale beached at Palm Beach on Queensland's Gold Coast on July 9, 2014.

negative effects. The popularity of whale-watching expeditions has led to some collisions between boats and whales, and the increased traffic on the seas has harmed whales and other marine life in other ways. The United States National Ocean Sanctuary Program has issued strict guidelines designed to protect whales and other marine creatures from overzealous sightseers.

chapter five
Today's Whale Populations

Whale populations are low. There are now only about 10,000 to 25,000 blue whales in the world. Although that may sound like a high number, it is much lower than the number of whales that existed before the dawn of modern whaling. The gray whales are not doing any better. The good news is that they are no longer listed as endangered because their worldwide population has recovered. However, they have disappeared from the Atlantic Ocean and now live only in the Pacific Ocean. There, they number only about 20,000.[1] Both blue and gray whales continue to need strong protection.

Of the other whales, the northern right whale is the most endangered. There are fewer than 1,000 of these whales swimming in our oceans. Despite being protected, they are showing few signs of recovery and are very rare in the eastern North Atlantic and North Pacific Oceans. The southern right whale, though not as endangered, has still greatly decreased in number. There are about 7,000 southern right whales today. There were between 60,000 and 100,000 before the species was hunted.[2]

There are only about 8,500 bowhead whales, but that species is showing signs of recovery.[3] At the time of the commercial whaling moratorium in 1986, the number of bowhead whales had dropped to about 7,000—just more than half of their population before they were widely hunted.[4] Some subsistence hunting of the bowhead is allowed, but the number of whales killed each year is low, and recovery has not been affected. (Subsistence hunting of a species is

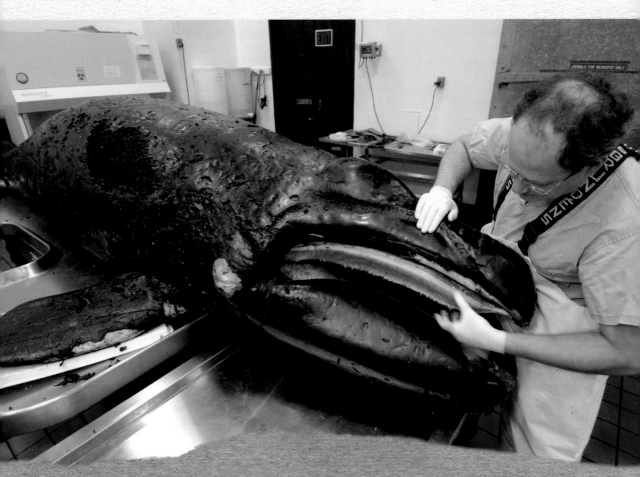

This scientist is examining a northern right whale calf to determine the cause of its death.

hunting done by people not for sport or for profit but because they depend on that species for their survival.)

The humpback whales, which are known for their elaborate songs, number around 20,000. There were originally 150,000 of these whales. While they are showing some positive signs of recovery, the humpbacks are still very vulnerable.[5]

There are currently around 80,000 sei whales and somewhere between 50,000 and 90,000 fin whales. These numbers are also well below historical levels. Neither of these endangered whale species is showing signs of recovery, but there is hope that both species will come back if measures to protect them are closely followed.[6]

Killer whales are currently in serious decline along the northwestern coast of the United States. Their numbers have dropped, mostly because there are few chinook salmon, which are their favorite prey. Killer whales, like other whales, have also suffered from contamination by PCBs. The many whale-watching boats that come into their breeding grounds may also be interrupting their reproductive processes. Due to its small size, this population of killer whales was listed as endangered under the Endangered Species Act in 2005 and designated critical habitat in 2006.[7]

Troubles for Whale Conservation

The recovery of many whale species has been slowed by nations that continue to hunt whales despite having signed nonhunting agreements. Perhaps the worst case of this was brought to public

When artificial sounds are added to the seas, researchers believe whales, who use sound to navigate, are further threatened. This whale is a killer whale.

Fast Fact!

Sadly, many whales are injured or die each year when they collide with large ships.

attention after the breakup of the Soviet Union. Several former Soviet government officials admitted in the 1990s that Soviet whaling vessels had been violating the moratorium on whaling for decades and had killed thousands of whales.

While Soviet ships practiced whaling in secret, a few nations have resumed whaling openly. Japan is the most prominent nation to have started whaling again. Whale meat is considered a delicacy in Japan, and scrimshaw, a type of carving done on whalebone, has long been a part of Japanese culture.

Japan defends its hunting of whales as scientific research by saying it needs to know whether whale populations are depleting the country's fish stocks. Critics say the Japanese are hunting whales because people are willing to pay high prices for whale meat. In 2014, the International Court of Justice ordered Japan to stop its whaling program.[8]

Norway has killed several hundred minke whales since 1992 and still exports whale parts to Japan. This trade continues today even though it is prohibited by the international agreements Norway has signed.

At meetings of the IWC, there have been fierce disagreements between nonwhaling nations and those nations that want to

Protesters in London voice their concerns about whaling.

continue hunting whales. The United States has threatened economic sanctions against both Japan and Norway to stop their whale hunts but has not taken any action so far. In the mid-1980s, an international boycott of Iceland's fish forced that country to stop whaling. In 2006, Iceland resumed commercial whaling.[9]

These countries are killing large whales that are protected by international agreements. But many small whales, including dolphins and porpoises, are still hunted in large numbers because they are unprotected.

Subsistence Whaling

Under IWC rules, subsistence whaling is permitted in Canada, Denmark, Greenland, the Russian Federation, St. Vincent and the Grenadine Islands, and the United States. One American Indian group, the Makah tribe of Washington State, even has a treaty with the United States government that allows the Makah to take whales. For many years, the Makah hunted gray whales, but their hunts were stopped while gray whales were an endangered species. Now that gray whales are no longer listed as endangered, the Makah hunt is again allowed. The tribe may currently take up to five whales per year.[10]

Whales and the Future

Whale sanctuaries—areas where all hunting of whales is forbidden—may be the best hope for whale recovery. The International Whaling Commission has created sanctuaries in the Indian Ocean and the Southern Ocean surrounding Antarctica. Several countries, including the United States, Australia, New

Humans are the reason blue whales are endangered. But we can help them make a triumphant comeback by reducing or eliminating our destructive behaviors.

Zealand, Tonga, Brazil, and the Cook Islands, have also established sanctuaries in their own waters.

There are many ways that people can help to protect whales. They can write to their government representatives and tell them that more needs to be done to protect whales. They can make changes in their everyday lives that will protect whales, including recycling more and throwing away less garbage so that trash will not someday end up in the oceans. They can also avoid dumping oil or other chemicals into the ground or down drains so that those products do not end up in local waterways.

Because humans are the biggest threat to whales' survival, we have in our hands the power to ensure that whales will flourish in the future. If we honor these magnificent creatures with our respect and care, they may well recover and swim the seas in great numbers as they did just two centuries ago. How wonderful it would be to look forward to seeing them for generations to come!

Good News for California's Blue Whales

As of 2014, the endangered California blue whale population has rebounded. There are as many blue whales living there now as there were before humans started decimating their numbers at the turn of the twentieth century.[11] The 2,200 blue whales are part of a conservation success story.

Chapter Notes

Chapter 1. The Largest Animal

    1. Nigel Bonner, *Whales of the World* (London: Blandford Press, 1998), p. 46.

    2. Roger Payne, *Among Whales* (New York: Charles Scribner's Sons, 1995), pp. 24–25.

    3. "Blue Whales," *National Aquarium in Baltimore,* n.d., <http://seaworld.org/animal-info/animal-infobooks/baleen-whales/diet-and-eating-habits> (January 28, 2015).

    4. "Blue Whale," *American Cetacean Society Fact Sheet,* n.d., < http://acsonline.org/fact-sheets/blue-whale-2/> (January 27, 2015).

    5. Payne, p. 269.

    6. "Baleen Whales, Diet and Eating Habits" *SeaWorld Parks and Entertainment,* n.d., <http://www.marinemammalcenter.org/learning/education/whales/blue.asp> (January 27, 2015).

Chapter 2. A Look at the Whale

    1. Dr. Anthony R. Martin, *The Illustrated Encyclopedia of Whales and Dolphins* (London: Salamander Books, 1990), p. 10.

    2. Ibid.

    3. Ibid.

    4. Ibid., p. 11.

    5. Ibid., p. 10.

    6. Nigel Bonner, *Whales of the World* (London: Blandford Press, 1998), p. 32.

    7. Ibid., p. 27.

    8. Ibid., pp. 37–38.

    9. Martin, p. 12.

    10. Bonner, p. 43.

    11. Ibid., p. 32.

    12. Ibid.

13. Ibid., p. 29.

14. Ibid., p. 32.

15. Martin, p. 68.

16. Ibid.

17. Bonner, p. 32.

18. Martin, p. 68.

19. Roger Payne, *Among Whales* (New York: Charles Scribner's Sons, 1995), p. 49.

20. Martin, p. 68.

21. Ibid., p. 70.

22. Payne, p. 24.

23. Ibid., pp. 34–35.

24. Ibid., pp. 49–50.

25. Ibid., p. 51.

Chapter 3. Threats to the Whale

1. Nigel Bonner, *Whales of the World* (London: Blandford Press,1998), pp. 61–62.

2. Roger Payne, *Among Whales* (New York: Charles Scribner's Sons, 1995), p. 253.

3. Ibid., p. 255.

4. Ibid., pp. 254–258.

5. Ibid., pp. 303–304.

6. Ibid., pp. 304–305.

7. Ibid., pp. 173–174.

Chapter 4. Watching Out for Whales

1. Roger Payne, *Among Whales* (New York: Charles Scribner's Sons, 1995), pp. 274–276.

2. Office of Protected Resources, "Cetaceans: Whales, Dolphins, and Porpoises," *National Oceanic and Atmospheric Administration,* n.d., <http://www.nmfs.noaa.gov/pr/species/mammals> (January 27, 2015).

3. International Whaling Commission. Conservation and Management, 2015, <https://iwc.int/conservation> (January 28, 2015).

4. Ibid.

5. Ibid.

6. Payne, pp. 222–223.

Chapter 5. Today's Whale Populations

1. World Wildlife Fund, "Great Whales in the Wild," n.d., <http://www.worldwildlife.org/species/blue-whale > (January 27, 2015).

2. Ibid.

3. Ibid.

4. Roger Payne, *Among Whales* (New York: Charles Scribner's Sons, 1995), p. 269.

5. Ibid.

6. World Wildlife Fund.

7. NOAA Fisheries., "Killer Whale," January 15, 2015. <http://www.nmfs.noaa.gov/pr/species/mammals/whales/killer-whale.html" (January 27, 2015).

8. ABC News, "Japan Ordered to Immediately Stop Whaling in Antarctic as International Court of Justice Rules Program Was Not Carried Out for Scientific Purposes," March 31, 2014, <http://www.abc.net.au/news/2014-03-31/ijc-japan-whaling-southern-ocean-scientific-research/5357416> (January 27, 2015).

9. BBC News, "Iceland 'Breaks Ban on Whaling," October 22, 2006, <http://news.bbc.co.uk/2/hi/europe/6074230.stm> (January 27, 2015).

10. U.S. Department of Commerce News, "Fisheries Service Issues Draft Environmental Assessment on Makah Gray Whale Hunt, Sets Public Hearing," press release NOAA 01-R101.

11. Feltman, Rachel, "California Blue Whales Bounce Back From Whaling," *Washington Post*, September 5, 2014, <http://www.washingtonpost.com/news/speaking-of-science/wp/2014/09/05/california-blue-whales-bounce-back-from-whaling> (February 18, 2015).

Glossary

aboriginal—Having existed in a region from the beginning.

baleen—A hard hornlike substance in the upper jaws of baleen whales.

cetacean—Any member of aquatic marine mammals, such as whales, dolphins, and porpoises, that share certain traits.

commercial—Having to do with the buying and selling of goods.

conservation—The protection of plants, animals, and natural resources.

endangered—In danger of becoming extinct and not existing on earth anymore.

extinction—The death of an entire group, or species, of living things.

krill—Tiny creatures shaped like shrimp that are the main food for baleen whales.

migration—The movement of a large group of animals from one place to another.

moratorium—A legal stop or delay of a specific activity.

PCB—A chemical compound used in industry; it is toxic to animals.

pesticide—A chemical substance that is used to kill insects, animals, or unwanted plants.

population—The total number of people, animals, or plants living in a specific area.

predator—An animal that hunts and eats other animals for food.

species—A group of animals or plants that have similar features. They can produce offspring of the same kind.

threatened—A group of animals that is close to becoming endangered.

FURTHER READING

Books

Austin, Bryant. *Beautiful Whale*. New York: Harry N. Abrams, 2013.

Baillie, Marilyn, Jonathan Baillie, and Ellen Butcher. *How to Save a Species*. Toronto: Owlkids Books, 2014.

Bjorklund, Ruth. *Blue Whales*. New York: Scholastic, 2013.

Dembicki, Matt. *Wild Ocean: Sharks, Whales, Rays, and Other Endangered Sea Creatures*. Golden, Colo.: Fulcrum Publishing, 2014.

Miller-Schroeder, Patricia. *Blue Whales*. New York: Weigl Publishers, Inc., 2013.

Pringle, Laurence. *Whales!: Strange and Wonderful*. Honesdale, Pa.: Boyds Mill Press, 2012.

Rice, William. *Endangered Animals of the Sea*. New York: TIME for Kids Nonfiction Readers, 2013.

Web Sites

nmfs.noaa.gov/pr/pdfs/education/kids_times_whale_blue.pdf
Read all about the blue whale.

seaworld.org/animal-info/animal-bytes/mammals/endangered%20whales
Learn about endangered whale species and their status.

worldwildlife.org/species/blue-whale
Wealth of information on endangered and threatened animals.

INDEX